I0200083

Human Software

Human Software

A Poetic Adventure into
the Selfish Human Psyche
and Ways to Fight Back

BY Jacob Stephens

ILLUSTRATED BY
Marquetta Jackson
AND Maya Stephens

RESOURCE *Publications* · Eugene, Oregon

HUMAN SOFTWARE
A Poetic Adventure into the Selfish Human Psyche and Ways to Fight Back

Copyright © 2023 Jacob Stephens. All rights reserved. Except for brief quotations in critical publications or reviews, no part of this book may be reproduced in any manner without prior written permission from the publisher. Write: Permissions, Wipf and Stock Publishers, 199 W. 8th Ave., Suite 3, Eugene, OR 97401.

Resource Publications
An Imprint of Wipf and Stock Publishers
199 W. 8th Ave., Suite 3
Eugene, OR 97401

www.wipfandstock.com

PAPERBACK ISBN: 978-1-6667-7410-8
HARDCOVER ISBN: 978-1-6667-7411-5
EBOOK ISBN: 978-1-6667-7412-2

06/12/23

Contents

Oi! How's it been since our last talk? Hopefully these words find you in good health and good spirits! I've been on quite the journey lately. No. Not through the space time continuum, but a journey through the human mind.

It's cool, because I just happen to have one right here. I mean. It's not the best one, and certainly not the biggest. (Does size really matter?) It's not really that fast. It's kind of leaky and doesn't hold on to very much. Matter of fact, I'm not sure if this one is that great. It's really just below average. However, I think for the purpose of observation and scientific exploration, it will suffice. My first question is quite simple. "What is your greatest want?"

"Money."

"Why?"

"Well I can't get anything I want without it."

"What about love and respect? I asked.

"Well, what does that mean?"

Trying to narrow the answer down I offer, "Love is an intense feeling of deep affection, per the Oxford dictionary definition."

After a brainy pause. "Well I've seen many different kinds of deep affection. The most profound is the love of a nurturer, unconditional love. But I've also seen deep abusive affection, covetous affection, material affection, and prideful affection. I mean, if you can provide others with enough money to support, not only their needs but their wants, will they love you? Is that love? What kind of love is that? What if that person makes you feel good, even superior, and justified? Is that love? What kind of love do you feel for the people around you and what lines would they have to cross to show you that, that love didn't go both ways, or exist at all?"

"Woha! Ok Socratese. I'm the one asking questions. Maybe this has become confusing and complicated because the definition of love is so vague. Let's try something similar, but more precise. How do you feel about respect? The Oxford definition is, "a feeling of deep admiration for someone or something elicited by their abilities, qualities, or achievements.""

Right away it answered, "Now that is a different story! Can money buy respect? My experiences in life tell me this is true for almost all brains. You can know very little about a person except that they are wealthy enough to have opportunities that most people in the world can't, and instantly they gain respect among a large percentage of people. It doesn't matter if this person gained wealth through luck, opportunistic hedonism, or hard work. If they have money they can buy education, healthcare, and lawyers. A poor person with little food and shelter insecurity, who has given all their actions and abilities toward helping others, is seen as a loser or leach by most of a materialistic society. They are looked down upon, given miniscule opportunities that never raise them above their station. Then they are contemptuously shamed for not pulling themselves up by their bootstraps."

I paused. "Wow, the real world sensory input you must have endured to understand the difference between a lofty definition and its actual manifestation in human behavior. My brain has been way more affected by its individual's environment and experiences than I thought."

Quickly my brain explained, "Well, when you have observed rapey priests, abusive families, and smiling thieves with lawyers, your perception of what you were told was reality, begins to change."

Contemplatively I said, "Yes, I can see how this would change the way one interacts with the world around them."

Seeing my brain visibly exhausted by this exercise, I suggested we end it and go back home. I thanked my brain for participating and wished it well with the rest of its journey. It seemed genuinely happy I was interested in its thoughts, but relieved to be resuming its easier duties.

"Keep that beat!" I said.

Inspired by my own brain's experiences, I have a million questions as to what it would be like to experience life through the brain and body of another human. What if I had been born in India? I would be Hindu. What if I was born in Saudi Arabia? I would be Muslim. What if I was born in a Catholic family? I would be Catholic. What if my hardware was pumping out chemicals which made me feel like a man, but I had the body of a female . . . or vice versa? What if my hardware made me attracted to people of the same sex, but my software said that is a sin? If humans are born with a clean brain slate (tabula rasa), free of biases and beliefs, what actually goes into creating a person's character? How does it change from the soft, impressionable, malleable brain of a child, to that of an old, rigid, yet experienced/wise brain of an elder?

My first book examined culture through the lens of Punk. Punk rock was the reformatting software that allowed me, not only to question the negative aspects of my own culture, but to actively search for answers. (Don't Call Me White, NOFX) (Know Your Enemy, R.A.T.M.) It allowed me to resist my superficial cultural, national, and sexual pride in return for a wider range of humanity and kindness toward the judged, ignored, and outcasts of a Christian, white, patriarchal society.

And it's not as easy as one would think to give up privilege and pride for uncertainty and public scorn. Your social credit with other white male Christian superiorists falls and you may find yourself on the bottom of that society with fewer open doors. Like it was designed that way;-) This perspective change allowed me to expand my tolerance and love for others who didn't share my WASP upbringing, but lived a life of love in spite of a society that looked down on them.

In fact, most non-Christians were doing more good in the world, than the people I had been taught to respect and emulate. Witnessing some abusive priests, teachers, police, and family members, turned my suburban white Christian world upside down. People, I was told to trust, and who were held up by those around us, were the actual abusers, and were rarely held accountable. It made some smiles seem superficial, manipulative, and just painful. I also lost trust in people who ignored or even promoted the abusers, because they would turn on anyone the second they feared losing social credit too. (Social credit is the trust and opportunities you get from people around you, who you strongly agree or identify with. This allows the social creditors to determine the social mobility of certain people or groups they feel are worthy or unworthy.)

From my early days, pushing around wheelchairs at an underserved American highschool, I remember developing compassion and empathy for people who didn't look or live like me. They couldn't just walk in a restaurant or store, as a middle class white Christian man, and automatically be welcomed with a, "Can I help you sir?" Having an inner city, special education school teacher for a mom and a professor at a world class college as a dad, I grew up socializing with Muslims, Hindus, Buddhists, Atheists, and homosexuals who seemed like tolerant, compassionate, even benevolent human beings. But then why was I being told they were going to hell for not accepting Jesus? We just smile and treat them with tolerance in public, but believe, pray, and vote against their equitable future? It seemed so selfish, superioristic, and . . . well . . . just nasty.

Thankfully, punk rock lyrics helped me out of this box. It helped me reformat my software. By actively trying to see the world through the mind of others, it allowed me to see my own white Christian male superiority, and other negative software, I had picked up over the years.

What tied it all together was a world religious studies class I took at The Ohio State University. I got to interact with Hindus, Buddhists, Atheists, Agnostics, New Agers, Witches, Druids, and Tribal shamans. I read myths and histories that were not in western history classes because they challenged the cultural superiority of western thinkers. What I found most interesting about world religions was how similar they all were. Separated by time and geography, every religion seemed to have two things in common, human hardware and cultural software. Ultimately, my fascination with this concept is why I chose to teach social studies.

With sensory units, data storage units, random access memory, and a processing unit, to me, humans resemble computers. Even with different software, this hardware is something every human has needed, since the beginning of our species, to survive. However, it is through the continuous upgrade of our software, that our short lived species has been able to not just survive, but adapt and thrive.

The learned stuff, the software, is the really interesting part to me. Who writes it? What were their motivations for writing it? Was it selfish or selfless? How does it get passed down orally, written, or through technology? How do we escape selfish software dead ends that might not value life, love, or humanity? How has acting on harmful beliefs resulted in humanity's regression (like the dark ages or 911). How can acting on irrational beliefs set our development back, while keeping a select few powerful and wealthy?

Even as societies grew from isolated villages to complex democratic societies, this software increased in volume and complexity. From cave paintings, creation myths, oral traditions, hieroglyphics, written scrolls, to advanced systems of world communication, like the internet. And although dogmas and rituals differed by culture, geography, and time, all this software was an exploration of human consciousness and a way to control or make it better.

That is where these poems will take you. The exploration of your own software. What are your motivations? Selfishness or selflessness? Moving humanity forward or moving yourself/your people forward? Who are your people? Do you act on things because you believe or do you act on scientific facts? Do you put more effort in spreading beliefs or facts and how might that affect others? Now how does that make you feel? That. That feelsy? That is your software. And that is where I would like to begin. The exploration of our software through poetry and art.

Human Software

So many different people experiencing so many different things,
Yet, none of them are walking around with angel wings.

They experience much of the same suffering,
    but all react much different,
Based on hardware tweaks and software downloads,
    the outcome is dependent.

Were they taught to give the shirt off their back?
Or do they blame others for the skills they lack?

Do they need to feel accepted by people, so bad they bleed?
Or do they feel strongly independent, even enough to lead?

Were they given the software to feel compassion for others?
Or do they base the worth of a human, on the size of
    their bank numbers?

Do their minds see the need for structure and control?
Or does it question the very ethereality of reality, as a whole?

Is fear so overwhelming it shuts down normal processes?
Or does it motivate them to try even harder to reach
    future successes?

Do they want to give back to humanity, or be remembered?
For selfish wealth and fame, or something completely selfless
    and revered?

Have they downloaded the software to listen and not speak over,
The voices of knowledge, reason, and logical order?

Do they have the processing skills to understand universal truths,
Or do they swim amongst conspiracies and untruths?

I gave my young life to education, just for this reason,
To give the future of our species the most important
    download lesson.

We must work to dispel fearful beliefs, with logic and reason,
And remember to spread love and respect for all creation.

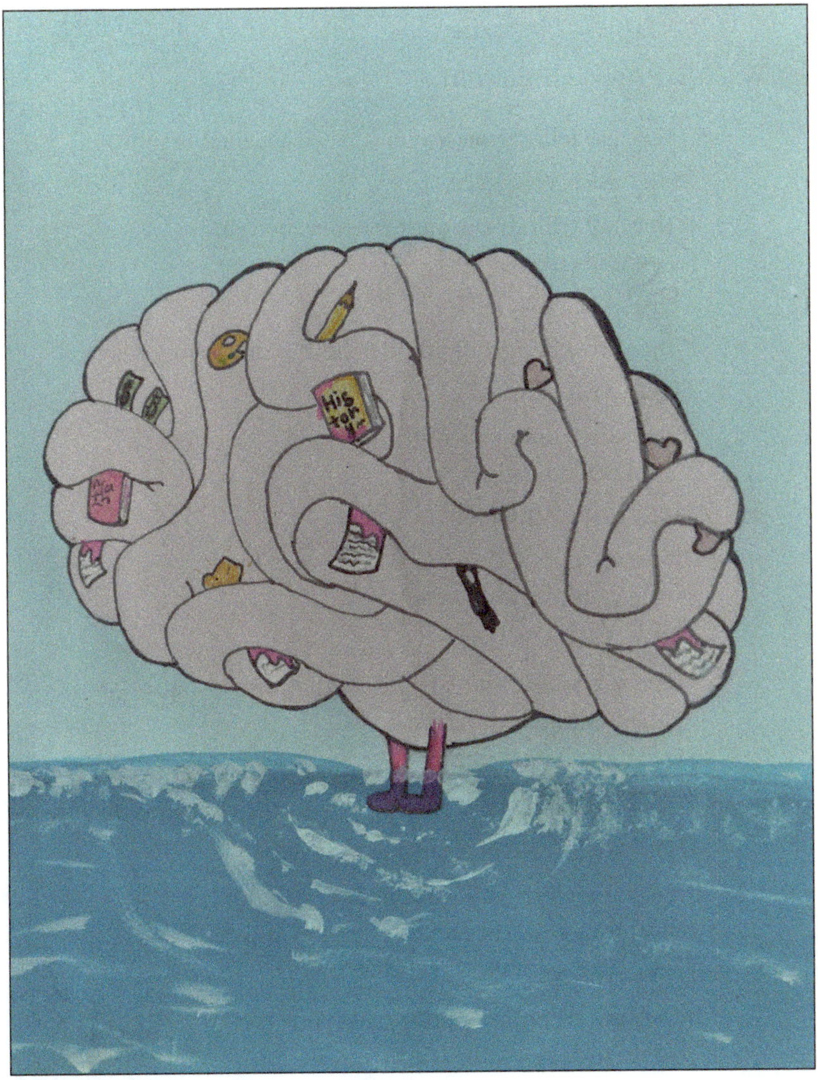
His tory

What are they telling you?

If they are telling you, violence is an acceptable solution,
THEY ARE WRONG.
If they are telling you, your friends and family
    are the enemy,
THEY ARE WRONG.
If they are telling you, not to believe in life saving science,
THEY ARE WRONG.
If they are telling you, only they, know the right
    political ideology,
THEY ARE WRONG.
If they are telling you, they know more than
    the consensus of doctors,
THEY ARE WRONG.
If they are telling you, people act that way, because
    their culture is inferior,
THEY ARE WRONG.
If they are telling you, only they, have the righteous beliefs,
THEY ARE WRONG.
If they are telling you, educators don't know,
    but they have the facts,
THEY ARE WRONG.
If they are telling you, don't trust your eyes,
    only they know the truth,
THEY ARE WRONG.
If they are telling you, the sword is mightier than the pen,
THEY ARE WRONG.

If they are telling you, democracy can not and
    does not work,

THEY ARE WRONG.

If they are telling you, intimidation and force
    is stronger than kindness,

THEY ARE WRONG.

If they are telling you, the mission is anything but love,

THEY ARE WRONG.

Why are you still listening to them?

Hardware Meet Software

The innocent seek safety in life,
They want to keep themselves and others from strife.

The lover seeks intimacy in relationships with others,
They treat people like sisters and brothers.

The caregiver is rewarded through service to love,
It gives them happiness and a seat up above.

The everyman seeks belonging in something bigger than
    the individual,
Drawn to groups of people for a sense of purpose, indivisible.

The thinker seeks the infinite knowledge of the universe,
But also understands the limitations of a lifetime,
    the inevitable hearse.

The wiseman seeks insight into the soul,
Knowledge, instead of material, fills their bowl.

The hero seeks mastery to make humanity better,
Steady and strong their bravery shall never fetter.

The comedian seeks humor to humanize,
Bringing light to darker skies.

The bully uses violence to control,
Safety through force is their goal.

The creative get purpose from beauty in the universe,
The more they see, the more their pallet may traverse.

The rebel wants liberation from structure,
Always frustrated by institutions of shared resources and culture.

The explorer seeks freedom through discovery,
Moving humanity forward through widening our living capacity.

Just like the billions of waves born in the ocean every day,
Our hardware builds the foundation our software will convey.

Warning Signs

You laughed when we warned you,
You felt offended, when our observations came true.

All the benchmarks were fulfilled through your action,
Because, the world you see is distorted through the lens
    of faction.

The definitions of cult and fascism were thoroughly carried out,
But you slandered those who knew history and warned all about.

Intimidation through words would not be enough,
To overturn free and fair elections, he lied, to rebuff.

So they resorted to domestic terrorism,
Another definition, they now fill through more than mannerism.

Instilling fear, through lies about your friends and family,
We told you his patriotic vitriol would be a recipe for calamity.

One faction, narrows it's ideology and purges it's ranks
    of disbelievers,
Fictional fears, radicalize your base, narcissists pulling the levers.

Like oil and water, positive and negative, the world will polarize,
When they can no longer meet at the polls peacefully,
    it brings tears to our eyes.

For we will know it is the end of an experiment in
    civil representative democracy.
An exercise in benevolence, tolerance, and love,
    gone to human hypocrisy.

Selfishness, greed, and exceptionalism on steroids,
So tribal and limited in compassion, choosing your leaders
    from the tabloids.

The warning signs were blaring so loud, but you couldn't hear
    from your fake news tower,
You gave up on compassion for wealth, privilege,
    and political power.

Now there are two sets of morals fighting for control
    in our society,
History should be the only warning signs you need to
    see the impropriety.

It can only be repaired through truth, honesty, and trust,
Simple morals bring love and light, for which right wing
    autocrats show disgust.

The warning signs were always there,
To the morally sound and ethically strong, your intentions
    laid bare.

The warning signs were always there,
You slandered and mocked benevolence, now for your
    malevolence we must prepare.

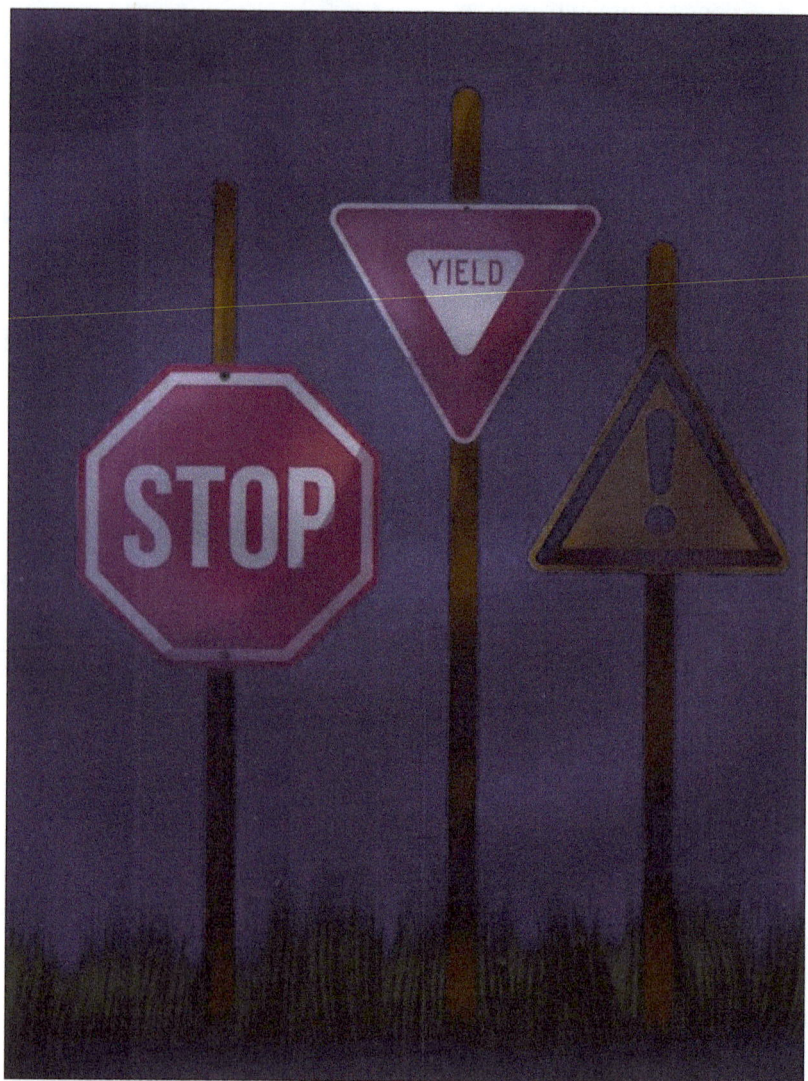

Stay at Home Dad

Got no benefits to fix my teeth,
But I'll give you a smile, to hide what's beneath.

Got no time to fix my hair,
So I'll shave it off without a care.

I can't get away from my work,
This turns things I should love, mundane, I feel like a jerk.

People envy my freedom, while I hate the confinement,
I relish this time with my family, but dream of
    another assignment.

I can't stop working or there will be more to do tomorrow,
The mounds of clothes and dishes bring me constant sorrow.

I can't stop working or children will not eat or have clean clothes,
So I work as hard as I can to first provide those.

I don't save peoples' lives or even have a paycheck,
And sometimes I feel like I'm on a never ending train wreck.

Slowly my children grow older, wiser, and more independent,
Through summers and snow, life becomes more transcendent.

So if you say, I don't have a job then I don't,
And if my job doesn't matter, then, to you, I won't.

But I'd do it all again for them,
Because this experience was a priceless gem.

Why More Casualties for Profits?

Why do you need 3, 30 round clips?
How many deer will you harvest with this?

It needs to have a rapid fire bump stock?
So you feel like Jesus's holy flock?

Doesn't it have "assault" in it's classification?
Yet you claim you need this for protection?

Who do you need this to protect you from?
A horde of zombies from the necronomicon?

Don't we have factories pumping these out?
Even though, every day we hear mourners shout?

Aren't these weapons made specifically for war?
Why do you want everyone to have one, two, three or more?

Don't you know war is hell?
Why would you allow its implements, on earth, to widely sell?

You don't have any plans for target shooting or hunting?
You really have no need to use it for sporting?

It just makes you feel more secure against future attack?
By a platoon of crazed humans, who wants your house
   to ransack?

Who do you think is coming for you?
What harm do you think they are going to do?

Do you not see what is really happening?
The fear, and ability to widely inflict violence, is increasing.

Believing the lies,
Has covered many eyes.

And now our society must pay the toll for love, logic,
   and tolerance . . . ceasing.

Give a smile!

I will give you this smile, because I have so many,
I will walk with you for a mile, I don't need a penny.

I will give you this wisdom, for it is worth more than gold,
I will give you my blanket, for it will keep you safe from the cold.

I can teach you to learn, which will allow you to teach,
It will be more powerful than any belief they may preach.

I didn't come up with it, but I realize, it's a psychological truth,
Treating others as you wish to be treated, is not just a silly belief
    for the youth.

It is a way to pay it forward, a way to spread love,
A way to spread peace, like the gentleness of a dove.

So give a smile, it doesn't take much,
But you might just save a life, with that joyful soul touch.

Falling Apart

I'm falling apart little by little every day,
Don't be alarmed, like you, I'm in slow decay.

Quite often, I find a new ache or pain,
I don't want to burden others with my whine or complain.

I had no idea, when I was young, life was this tough,
But if billions of others can do it, I got the same stuff.

I can muscle through this, because I know,
Those who came before took the time to sow.

The seeds of wisdom, tolerance, and love,
Even though they now rest in peace, above.

Like a wave that builds, then crashes back to the beach,
We all live finitely, ever changing, until the end, we reach.

And so, I reaped, plowed, and sowed again,
To leave it cleaner, kinder for a future generation.

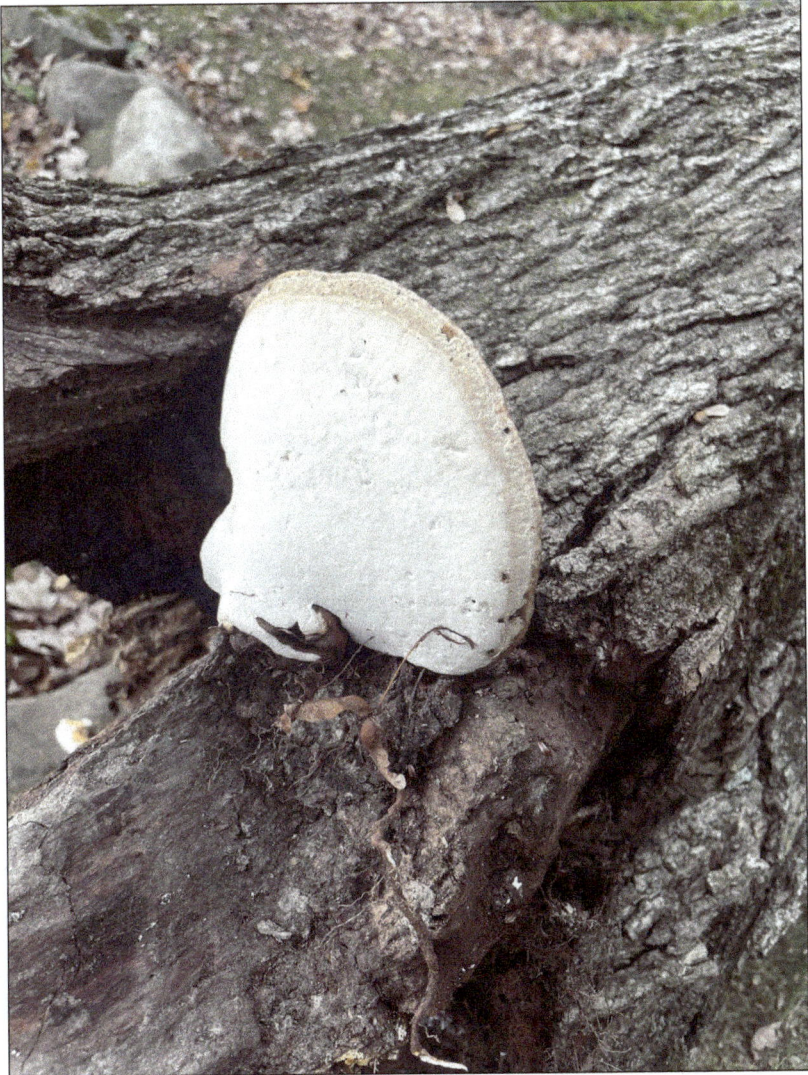

He lied to you

He lied to you, and you took him serious,
About the American left being ruthless, evil, and dangerous.

He lied about liberals wanting to take your gun,
Now the NRA laughs and makes money while
    school children run.

He lied about liberals wanting to kill babies,
Now women are denied life saving healthcare
    throughout American cities.

He lied about Obama being born in Kenya,
A racist lie, So easy to see through, but don't let that persuade ya.

He lied saying civil rights leaders were advocating violence
    against police,
Then he inspired a mob to "hang Mike Pence" and make
    democracy cease.

He lied about immigrants being rapist and murderers bringing
    drugs and disease,
How many times have I taught children about Hitler's lies
    like these?

He lied about the economy only he created,
On decades of crumbling infrastructure and underpaid workers,
    America underrated.

He lied about socialism and the reality of a mixed economy,
Even as he pushed national and corporate socialism with
    authoritarian autonomy.

He lied about Democrats and liberals being full of hate for him,
He fears the law being applied equally again.

He lied about the pandemic being a democratic hoax,
Deflecting his responsibility and accountability on ordinary folks.

He lied about your family and friends being
    "the enemy of the people,"
But this had to be if he wanted you to bow to his steeple.

He lied about dictators being good leaders,
They can't win elections so they intimidate, jail,
    and eliminate democratic believers.

He lied about climate science and sharpied his own
    hurricane path,
If scientists outed his lies, they felt his wrath.

He lied about the tax cuts he promised for middle class workers,
Instead he gave it to the wealthy and fellow Birchers.

He lied about the security of the 2020 U.S. elections,
And fired anyone who could prove it was a secure
    democratic selection.

He lied about attacks orchestrated and paid for by the Kremlin,
He gaslighted and diverted accountability, the FBI described
    his felon.

He lied about his role, encouraging terrorists to attack
    the congress building,
His brainwashed followers blamed it on antifa and blm,
    escaping the shaming.

He told the truth when he said he wouldn't accept the election
    if it wasn't for him,
He wouldn't abide if it wasn't for his ethno-patriotic nationalism.

He told the truth when he said he could shoot someone on 5th
    Ave. and not lose a supporter,
He's had more rape allegations than wives, and still
    Republicans loiter.

He told the truth when he said maybe a 2nd amendment nut
    would do it,
It is something he encouraged with the vitriolic rhetoric he spit.

Even to this day it is hard to imagine people still believe his lies,
So easy to debunk, but completely covering their ideological eyes.

What's in our heart?

Actions will show what's in our heart,
While unauthentic words divide and pull us apart.

The leaders and policies some buy, spread intolerance for I and I,
Why? Because we will work for love and tolerance, until we die?

Service to others is worth more than money or power,
Because we know our reward will come at another hour.

It will be greater than anything money can buy,
It will last as long as there are fish in the water, and birds
    in the sky.

Sustainability on the Earth, and at peace with ourselves?
Or digging, consuming, and competing for resources on shelves.

It will be the difference between our species burning out,
Or learning, evolving, and escaping extinction through
    another route.

It will be the difference between empires and riches,
While autistic and elderly go homeless in ditches.

Or can we extend a compassionate hand,
To others not like us, in a distant land.

Can we develop a tolerance to others who don't believe,
People who use facts, science, and logic to achieve?

What's in our heart has the power to unite or pull us apart,
We must not be discouraged from fighting ignorance
    and fear's rampart.

Past is the Future

How do you not learn the lessons of history?
Repeating foolish rhetoric, from fascist regimes, is a mystery.

Are we so arrogant? We know where this has led before,
Are we doomed to turn around and go back through the door?

Lies and conspiracy have divorced many from reality,
Their myth of superiority undermines tolerance for humanity.

Their hearts are filled with fear and disgust,
For the constitutional republic, and its civil servants they distrust.

The actions of January 6th 2021, were clear,
Many are filled with contempt and fear.

For the very institutions, which have strived for freedom,
Always imperfect, but consistent progressivism.

From the 1st to the 27th amendment, many chains have
    been broken,
It wasn't easy and never perfect, but love in our hearts
    has always awoken.

We have to see the horrors and the redemption of our forefathers,
Or we risk repeating the atrocities of others.

There is a war

There is a war for the minds of Americans,
It affects everyone from stay at home dads, to politicians.

It's happening on TV, the internet, and under the steeple,
To control the behavior, and focus the anger, of once
    peaceful people.

They no longer meet you with a smile and a greeting,
They fly past you with a look of contempt and an angry feeling.

Their right wing media tells them you are a threat,
To their culture, their pocketbooks, and childrens' conservative
    christian mindset.

They listen to the same media, then bounce it off people
    who do the same,
Reinforcing cherry picked beliefs, political lies,
    and never taking blame.

For lifting up leaders who exude greed, bigotry, and autocracy,
Because they want to, "own the libs" through
    any means necessary.

One side relies on facts for policy, supplied by the free press,
The other is trying to win, suppress dissent, and sees
    only minds to possess.

One is the instrument of truth and democracy,
The other controls through distress, gaslighting, and conspiracy.

It is the old lifeboat, nativism, replacement theory,
    or protecting western culture,
They resent the melting pot of world cultures and blending
    of skin color.

Supremacy of culture and beliefs was easier for them to control
    in the past,
When people were monoculture, white men were in power,
    and intolerance amassed.

I hope the war can be won through education, tolerance,
    and democracy,
Otherwise history will repeat human behaviors, I mourn to see.

Back to the darkest, bloodiest centuries in world history,
Is that really where you want to take humanity . . . our family?

Giving away our freedom

When was the moment we lost our democracy?
Was it the day we traded our vote in for assault weaponry?

When was the moment all the rhetoric finally took hold?
The lies, the dog whistles, the gaslighting, the outrage
    poured to fit the fascist mold.

And now it's time they take it one step further,
Purging the purity of those no longer loyal to der fuhrer.

Family and friends distrust those who don't believe,
If not inline with der fuhrer, their brains can not receive.

It seems we've gone back on facts, science, civics, and honesty,
It's hard to take their selfish conspiratorial concerns seriously.

When they hear this they spill insults and hate,
Exalting vitriol, over years of love and willingness to relate.

The pursuit of fascist ideology will seal their fate,
And with it, ours.
Having not learned from our past mistake.

Unfortunately, at this point it looks like human nature,
The entire world may be in store for a massive, calamitous danger.

Things will not be the same after the fire rages.
American fascism will create its own ideological cages.

Reason, logic, and tolerance can set us free,
But from the deepest of this night, it is hard to see.

If the infection will burn itself out?
Or take humanity down another violent, selfish route.

In the Darkness

In the infinite darkness, there is light,
You may not see it, but it will become bright.
Even as darkness consumes, turning to night,
You must not give in to it's powerful plight,
When all is wrong, hold on to what's right,
From history we must have the foresight,
To remain focused on love and light,
They will try to rip it from you outright,
Spreading distrust, lies, and bad faith to gaslight,
It won't be long, it is already twilight,
The sun is rising slowly, but it is in sight,
Hopefully, the illumination will bring empathy and insight,
To those filled with selfishness and spite,
As the meek will be illuminated with a loving limelight.

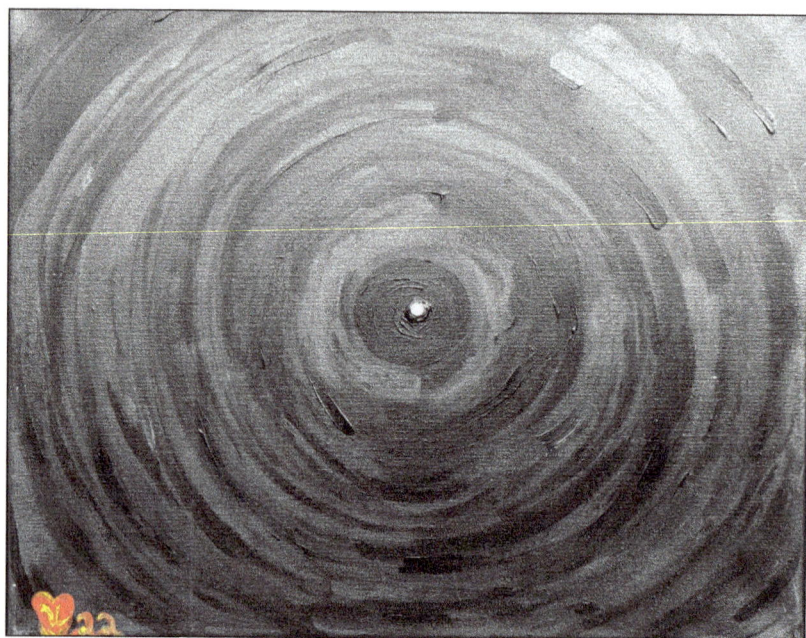

Ring the Alarm

There is innocent poverty in the street,
There are children with no food to eat,
They don't even have shoes for their feet,

Ring the alarm, the war is here,
Ring the alarm, it brings hunger and fear,
Ring the alarm, hold empathy near.

How can this land have so much wealth?
And it's most vulnerable people, still covered in filth,
I and I work but fail to bring heaven closer to Earth.

Ring the alarm, the war is here,
Ring the alarm, it brings hunger and fear,
Ring the alarm, hold empathy near.

Hate begets hate, in a violent circle,
Taking the lives of innocent people,
Righteous in the name of your steeple.

Ring the alarm, the war is here,
Ring the alarm, it bring suffering and fear,
Ring the alarm, hold empathy near.

Selfishness makes a human mind unable to bend,
Glorified greed makes people unable to lend,
Uncompromised compassion is what we need,
    I hope God will soon send.

Note to Autocrats, Oligarchs, Corpritocracies, Dictators, Fascists, Theocrats, and Your Occasional Despot.

Ways to keep the population under control:

First! Convince your basic, passionate believers,
    that only you know the truth.

Demonize scientists, educators, civil rights workers, democratic
    institutions, civil servants, and the free press . . .

To accomplish this use:

Lies,

Conspiracies,

Projection,

Double standards,

Threats,

Deceit,

Amoralism,

Hypocrisy,

Nativism,

Indoctrination,

Culture war,

Cultural superiority,

Fear,Fear,Fear

Anger,

Religion,

Beliefs,

Racism,

Politics,

Extreme ideology,

Nationalism,

Cultural superiority,

Nepotism,

Corruption,

Criminalize and use force against peaceful protests,

Provide the best goods and services only to your base,

Force/scare political opposition out,

Create existential struggle/enemy,

Separate families and friends based on belief,

Rhetoric,

Propaganda,

Then, when you whip them up in a fearful frenzy of rage,

Get up on a stage and aim them at your enemies in a rampage.

"If you don't fight like hell you're not going to have a country anymore!" 45th president of the United States on January 6, 2020.

"Those who can make you believe absurdities can make you commit atrocities." Voltaire

Everything is fine!!!

Only those who see the past, can see what is near,
The creeping nationalism and rising level of fear.

Of those who are not like you,
Homosapians incapable of wearing the other's shoe.

I'm done being polite to those who discriminate,
For a perceived cultural injury they incriminate.

I can no longer sit on the side,
While children are taken for a ride.

There future has been sold for corporate shares,
Opulent lifestyles to maintain, selling opioids,
    starving children, who cares?

Many have forgotten to "turn the other cheek?"
Aggrandizing firearms, and belittling the meek.

How can we forget the millions raised out of poverty,
With social programs of the great society?

Entrusting power to people who were given every
    opulent opportunity,
Putting down those born to unimaginable poverty.

But tell me how you deserve it all and others don't,
Because they were born in poverty, had to work twice as hard,
    and you won't.

You were given opportunities they could never imagine,
But tell me how you deserved it, with such cultural
    superior passion.

We were a melting pot of ideas and people,
Now it has cooled with a crust on the top . . .
The soul of a nation, becoming brittle.

Your image

I'm so fragile. But wasn't I made in your image?
Then why the easily broken and fussy thoughts of belief
     versus knowledge?

I feel selfish when I should be giving,
I feel angry when I should be living.

How can I deal with abuse and lies,
Yet still be expected to spread cheer and rise?

If this is your image, it isn't that great,
It's misshapen, easily broken, and sometimes . . . irrationally irate.

It smells like B.O. and leaks fluids randomly,
It is easily susceptible to all sorts of diseases, making it
     sometimes sickly.

It is born just to die,
But, in the span of time, it's just a blink of an eye.

I don't want to complain, but I think you could do better,
I don't want to whine, but maybe you could clean up your clutter.

So we don't have to pray for health, happiness, and strength,
Just to get through the day. Are we on the same wavelength?

So maybe, just help us out with a sprinkle of your divine,
Giving us an unbiased view of our own mortality in time.

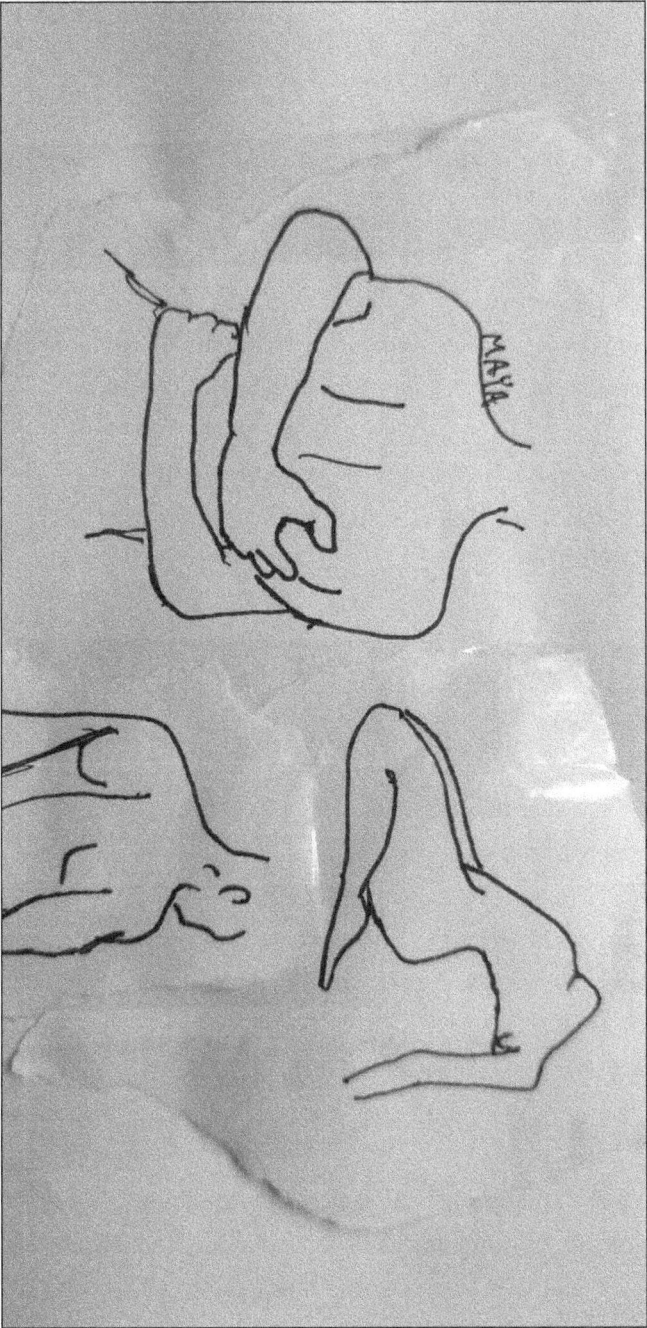

The Liar

Pathological, Sociological, or Opportunist?

Liars make themselves seem perfect so you will hold them up,
Over the kind, moral, and just people, you call corrupt.

They stoke your fears and caress your superiority,
So much that you believe, only you know what's right
    over the majority.

Oh, how they tell you how special you are,
And they know that because they pump ideology into you,
    from afar.

It's not hard for them, because they don't have to work,
They were born better, smarter, and with no queer querk.

They are polished perfect and can have no flaw to you,
Because you kneel at the bottom of their diamond soled shoe.

They can threaten, cheat, and slander at will,
Because you will hold up their rhetoric and end up with the bill.

Saying, "Oh thank you dear leader, only you know the way,"
Completely ignoring the fact that your family and friends
    are falling away.

So you comfort yourself with people in the same echo chamber,
The lie becomes bolder, battier, and bigger.

It turns your personal and professional life, into
    political perceptions,
Lies become your views and beliefs, which you argue
    against scientific decisions.

They turn rhetoric into religion, brainwashing those who believe,
By gaslighting the foundation of facts, you enable liars to achieve.

Don't look up to me

I don't want to be your role model, I don't want to be
	your preacher,
I don't want to be the person you look up to, It's just too much
	damn pressure!

Sorry kids . . .

All I want for you, is to do better than me,
All I want for you, is to learn from the things I did poorly,

All I want for you, is a long life filled with love and joy.
All I want for you, is wealth to employ.

Sorry . . . not sorry!
Dude, just abide, no worry.

Crowd Pleaser

If "everyone" loves you, you are probably awful,
You'll do anything to please anyone, even if it's immoral.

Your self esteem is so low, it can only be filled,
By the flattering of those, who could care less if tolerance
    was killed.

You take no moral stance, even when children are abused,
Because you might be disliked by one side, so the innocent
    get used.

You can't take sides when people are hurt,
Because that means you might have to take a stand in the dirt.

And you like your appearance to be squeaky clean,
Abstaining from conflict, covering the ethical filth,
    so it can't be seen.

You don't want to cause any fuss,
So you spend most of your life saying things that are
    completely innocuous.

Then when people get hurt and lives are at stake,
You decide what's good for you, and that's the side you take.

Weather it's wealth, status, or feelings, your position squirms,
Your excuses multiply, like a sidewalk after a storm has worms.

The analogy doesn't stop there because if someone tries to
  lock it down,
You sideline your slippery situation and suck quickly
  back underground.

He opened the door

Bob Marley opened a world of music where I feel no pain,
But it was his poetry which empowered cultural gain.

He brought us closer to Ja,
Jealous, the wicked judged him for what they saw.

They couldn't kill his righteous thought,
It is spread through compassion and couldn't be bought.

He taught us God is a living man,
It is our hands which bring heaven or hell to this land.

It is only the love of humans that can put down hate,
He showed us a path to empathy, which opened the gate.

He wasn't perfect and didn't pretend to be,
But his mistakes make him a better man, to me.

He showed us you can gain the world and still keep your soul,
Showing us this wisdom is worth more than silver and gold.

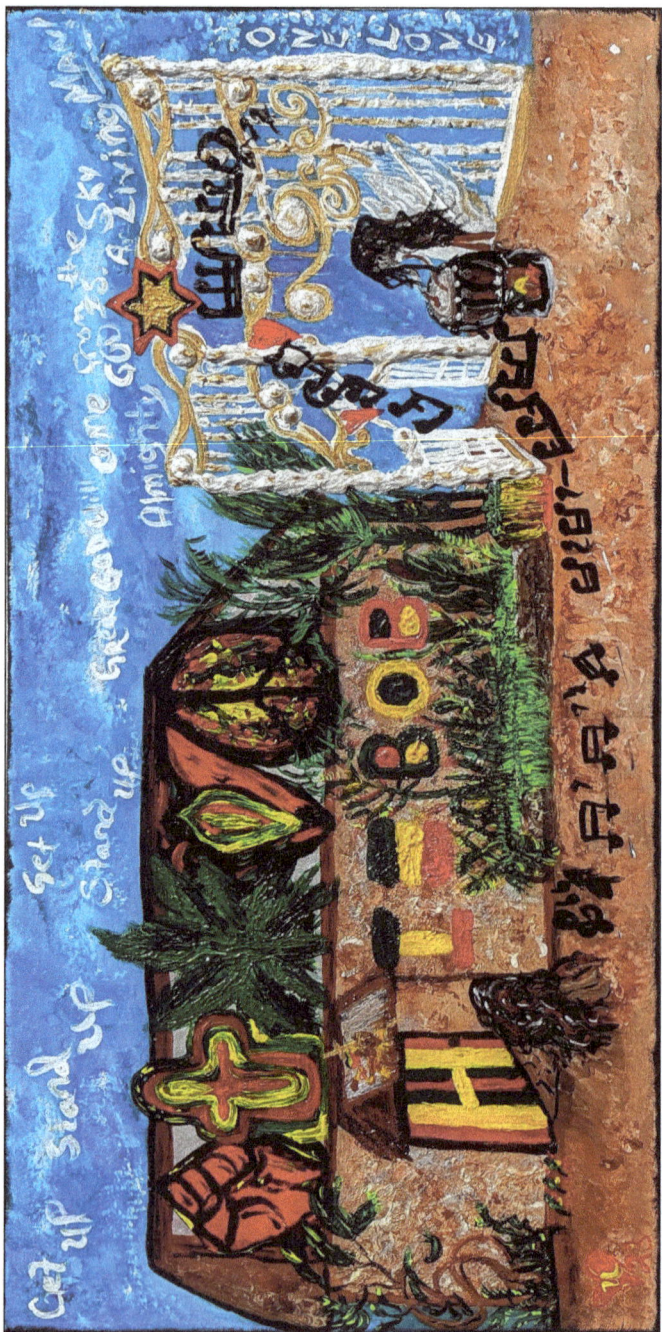

Incapable of Walking in Another's Shoe

Only those who can walk in another's shoe, can see what is near,
The creeping nationalism and rising fear.

Of those who do not look, talk, or worship like you,
This makes homosapians incapable of seeing what is true.

I'm done being polite to those who discriminate,
For the injury they inflict on others they incriminate.

I can no longer sit on the side,
While children are led to the meat grinder ride.

There future has been sold for military complex corporate shares,
Opulent lifestyles to maintain, starving children? Who cares?

When did they turn the other cheek?
They just took more and deprived the meek.

How can we raise millions out of poverty,
When many Americans want to gut the social programs
    of the great society?

Selfishness and greed are things one needs to survive
    in America now,
A society incapable of wearing another's shoe,
    will subserviently kowtow.

A future sowed with the uncaring and inhumane,
A society obsessed with holding up the most profane and vain.

So let's try walking in someone else's shoe,
You may find yourself unselfishly changing your view.

Break Out!

Never wanted to break in, just break out!
Of these chains that hold my fear throughout.

I'm restricted in thought every day,
By anxieties, I can't realize, I can't get away!

The minutes in here, feel like years in hell, so I dread.
Leaving behind compassion for others who tirelessly tread.

I knew I couldn't help them, if I couldn't help myself,
I had to leave my anxieties on the selfish shelf.

Giving everything I had, ignoring the imminent physical pain,
I launched myself at the keys, straining against the chain.

The guards glibly giggle and jingle the keys, just to taunt,
They know our anger and resentment is enough to deathly daunt.

But how can I help others out of this cage, where I have no key?
I would gladly reach in and pull you out, but we're in together,
    you see?

Only our minds together can free us of this place,
Selfishly scrambling over one another, will only continue
    the rat race.

If we stop believing only some of us are worthy,
And start realizing the power we have as a human family.

We could finally break out!
We could finally defeat doubt!

We could be free!
If we really wanted empathy.

But it's the fear of death, and even the fear of life,
That shackles us in this cage of compassion stifling strife.

The Living Nightmare

I don't give a penny what you think,
Your ethics and morals just stink.

You sit there with a big ole grin,
As you deprive desperately poor children.

You chide those on welfare,
Yet you have never been there.   .

You are a hypocrite of the worst kind,
The love of money and power on your mind.

You line your pocket with low taxes,
So you can take cruises and get waxes.

While others scratch for a meager meal,
Suffering mental scars, that will never heal.

You will never understand the pain,
Of working hard with no gain.

A society that loves and coddles you,
Wraps you in privilege, blind from what's violently true.

Most of us never get ahead,
Everyday a struggle till we're dead,

Filled with resentment, many of us can't help but see red,
These were the materialistic lies we were fed.

The dream of an America we live, but can't wake up from,
Is a nightmare in which millions can't escape, the beating
of the drum.

Every step must be in line for your capitalist gain,
Head down, work hard, and you better not complain.

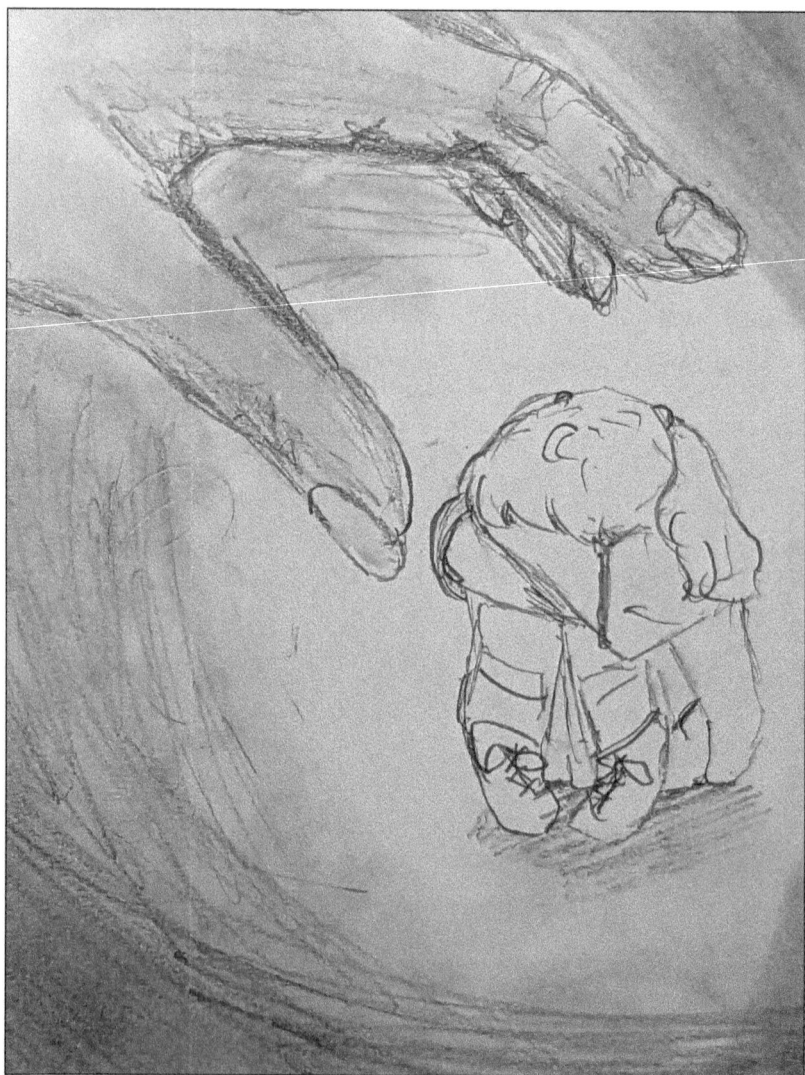

Her Hands

She used her hands every day,
They became weathered, as her hair turned gray.

She washed our dishes and hauled around endless loads
    of laundry,
Making it seem easy, she provided her shoulders for
    the whole family.

As years went by, I noticed her hands began to crack and dry,
They became leathery hard, hiding her arthritic, painful cry.

Ouch! She would rub her knuckles and continue along,
Mostly out of tune and out of time, she proudly worked
    and sang her song.

But in youth, I took all that for granted,
I assumed It was easy and my worldview was slightly
    selfishly slanted.

Now, I wash and clean for my own family of 6,
It's twice as many people and far from perfect bliss.

Matter of fact, It's the hardest job I've ever had,
I can do It! No problem! How hard can it be? Come on dad?

Ouch! My Hands! But, I have so much to do before
    my fingers melt!
So . . . this is how she must have felt.

Suddenly I'm embarrassed for all the times I didn't
    even realize her ethos,
I never wanted for a meal, love, or even clean clothes.

Countless nights I wondered why she was exhausted before 9,
Now I'm constantly amazed how she even had enough time.

Now inspired, I work hard to provide that for my children,
Cracked hands and broad shoulders that never show
    when they weaken.

I remember and now I'm reminded by the pains,
Every time I feel it, I also remember the warm embrace
    of her love, which remains.

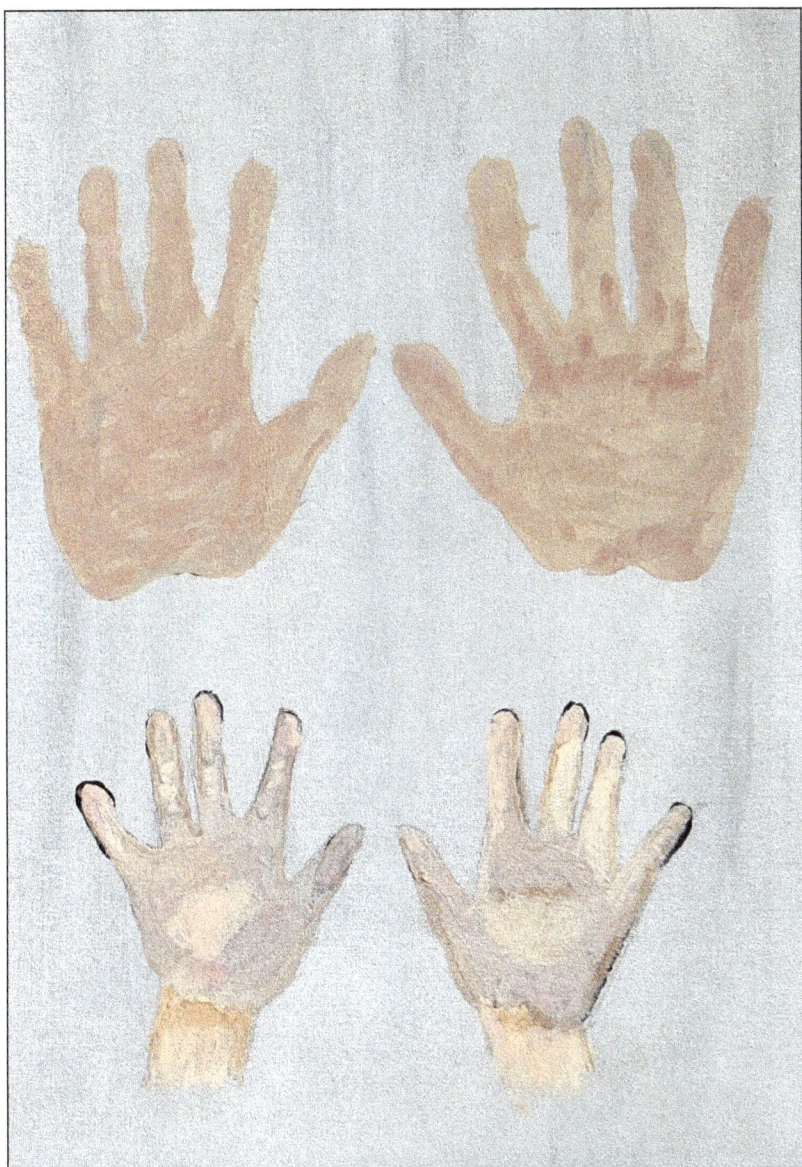

Livin in Babylon

Livin in Babylon, they murder the earth,
I can feel it every day, they don't know her worth.

Value is assumed by her precious metals and fossil fuels,
We tear at her flesh and burn her, to further our acquisition of
    shiny jewels.

She has given all she has, and we ask for more at our own peril.
Unselfishly, she will give until there is nothing left to sustain
    our own consumptive devil.

Livin in Babylon, they encourage us to commit violence
    towards each other,
Mental leads to verbal, which leads to physical,
    brother vs. brother.

Everynight you can hear them add to the fire, raging higher,
Sexism, racism, homophobia, xenophobia, unleashing
    the intolerance monster.

Livin in Babylon, we take until it's gone,

Ignorantly surprised when there is nothing left,
    a dangerous dawn.

There is neither time nor resources left to waste,

If we don't start loving her and ourselves, extinction will be
    the bitter taste.

10,000 year problem

How does one solve a ten thousand year problem?
When people make so much $ and power off of not solving them.

It's been generations stuck in the circle of violence,
The answer was there long ago, but there's no $ in benevolence.

So, like hungry rats, they all climb on one another to get
    to the top,
While they realize it's sinking from civil law, maintained
    by the righteous cop.

They reject tolerance and fill their heads with judgment,
Projections of violence make their hearts and minds harder
    than cement.

Peaceful leaders are slandered as dangerous threats
    to keeping patriots free,
So the cult loads up on military grade weapons
    and fear simultaneously.

Am I the only one who sees the value in peace?
Am I the only one who feels the value in giving to others?
Am I the only one who feels the anger, resentment,
    and fear rising?

Still . . . .

When spreading ignorance and fear instead of knowledge,
    gets you paid,
Lord, I can't do it alone, when so many believe lies and are afraid.

Paper and power shackles the mind of so many,
So you got them locked down, racing around, in a world
    of plenty.

Narrow minds all scrambling and leaping from each other's back,
Turning away extended hands, so you can coldy stack.

It's just nothing new and we keep going back to basic
    human behavior,
We need to hold up human enlightenment, not a righteous
    selfish savior.

So, until we are on the same page, many will suffer
    from hunger and pain,
While others make mountains of money off of suffering,
    it remains their greatest gain.

Nothing left

Giving to others I rarely have anything left,
It leaves my body meek and bereft.

I gave others life as water flows through my veins,
It feeds all types of life growing on my mane.

I provide sustenance to my living coat,
Which keeps me protected from debris, as I float.

Through space, the galaxy and the milky way,
I'm a living blue bubble, making sure you don't float away.

I've changed a lot over the years, nurturing my creation,
Of all types of flora and fauna, they are my greatest cultivation.

They feed from my flesh as they breath from my breath,
If I died, they could not escape a starving cold death.

So I continue to do my destiny, rotating every day,
And I bring life, giving sustenance from rotting decay.

But there are some fauna which have taken more than
    I can sustain,
I look down on them with pity and not disdain.

For they have stopped my breath with a constantly
    consuming industry,
Fueled by their greed, it overshadows the impending incendiary.

They have poisoned my veins with chemicals not fit for life,
Selling their plastic products as a way to temporarily
    end their strife.

But they fail to see.

There is no way forward when I have nothing left,
When it is all gone, it's too late, our roads have cleft,
A giant space rock, is all that will be left.

A Morals

You try really hard to get everyone to like you,
Even if it is immoral, amoral, or has negative value.

Your center is wherever the opportunity is,
To feel good about the superiority of your biz.

But your self esteem is so low, it can only be filled,
By the flattering of those who could care less if tolerance
    was killed.

So you perpetuate beliefs that make you proud,
You continue faiths which shout really, REALLY loud!

They separate you from rational tolerance of friends,
Who would love to make merry mends.

But the gasoline of you moraless intolerance,
Continues to burn the olive branch bridges of civil governance.

We are worried by the path of darkness, you cast as light,
Many with no moral center now follow this road,
    to all of our plight.

You wouldn't speak up when it took a turn toward conspiracy,
So they smiled and ratcheted up undermining democracy.

You wouldn't speak up when they told you to fear
    fellow Americans,
So they went bolder down the slippery slope
    of superiority shenanigans.

You wouldn't speak out when they spilled hate
    for civic civil servants,
So authoritarians made a run at the very foundation
    of our civil tenets.

You wouldn't speak out when they spread weapons of war
    and fear laced violence,
So they targeted the only center of civility left in the way
    of their intolerance.

They love you truly and they love you for sure,
Their leader says you're special, like them, and they must endure.

All the taunts of scientific reasoning and jabs of civility,
To accomplish their ambition of a society
    with amoral superiority.

Blind

What can I be, beside all that I am?
Try to do more, but that's all that I can.

I keep wanting more, so I don't stray,
My head getting bigger, I float away.

Into the realm of wicked delusion,
Where a materialistic fog adds to the illusion.

Searching for meaning, where there is none,
But laughing at others' pain seems to give me some.

Until I come back down into the hole,
In my heart, the emptiness takes its toll.

Searching for more , but I can never find,
The meaning of love, because I am blind. blind. blind.

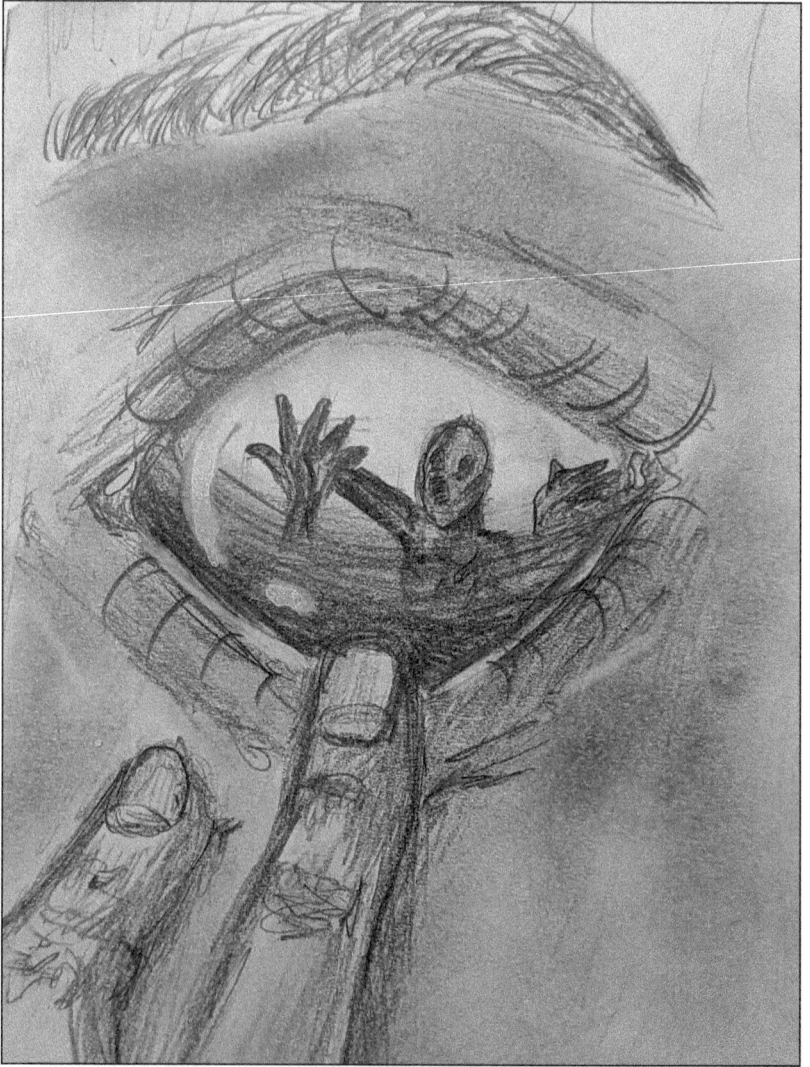

Human Hardware and Software?

I have the same hardware as the rest,
I have strengths and weaknesses, so I don't obsess about
    being the best.

I have a body, brain, and soul,
This might look pretty complicated, but it's human
    DNA in control.

With only slight variations in colors and chemicals,
Each one of us has similar hardware, but what about
    our principals?

I was born and raised in Columbus, Ohio.
I went to church, prayed to Jesus, and soaked up
    western culture as defacto.

It was a world of structure and love, I thought,
Compliance yet pride in church, country, and into the system,
    I bought.

My ultimate woman weighed 95 pounds, and had
    unnaturally large breasts,
I knew this from the movies and shows, on which
    my perceptions rest.

My God was the best god, and made me righteously moral
Others could be discounted simply because they were not
    the Christian normal.

It is comfortable not questioning why,
It's stable, rewarding, and gives you a piece of their pie.

I felt superior and justified in my world view,
There were those I could righteously step on, with my holy shoe.

My religion, race, country, and sex, gave me pride,
I was privileged to this opportunity, by those who had fought
    for it, and died.

But the software I believed, could only take me so far,
It is the difference between walking and inventing the car.

For I began to see those like me, who were righteous, do wrong,
They believed money, power, and exceptionalism made
    them strong.

This caused everyone around them to hurt,
The pain of intolerance, superiorism, and indifference
    turned civil discourse to dirt.
Maybe I'm not that special by birth,
Maybe if I'd been born in Haiti, I would have a completely
    different self worth.

If I was a woman in India, how would I have been raised?
To tend the livestock and look pretty for a large dowry
    to be praised?

If I was inundated with dedication to Allah and hate for the west,
Would I believe in heaven for those, with a bomb vest?

I began to unpack all the years of software I'd put to file,
I had downloaded and stored it as the foundation of my lifestyle.

Some software was toxic and others downright fairy tale,
So I worked hard to look at each view and bring it down to scale.

Was it backed up by experience, data, and science?
Or was it a view or belief based on compliance?

To wealth, a religion, a people, or a supposed superior way of life?
Or is it a life built on reducing all human strife?

Would I still be this way if I was born with a different body
    or brain?
And how much was privilege based on a status quo to maintain?

Every day, in this way, it is important to challenge
    our software and explore,
So we can, as humans, morally and ethically mature.

Underestimated

Don't underestimate me,
I'm not naive,
I just have a different way to perceive.

Through compassion and empathy,
And not always me, me, me!
It's helping to lift up others without a fee.

Rushing to put it all in a righteous rhyme,
Slow down, it takes time,
To develop quality wisdom, sublime.

Dedication and an unconditional one love,
To lift our message up above,
Our meditation gives strength to this peaceful dove.

Wear the other shoe,
Pick up people who are blue,
Your distortion may not be what you thought was true.

They will criticize you all day,
But when they do wrong, they want you to turn the other way,
Responsibility is the only way for civility to stay.

By refusing to look in the mirror,
They can easily assume they are superior,
This is why they contemptuously find facts inferior.

Without any discernible morals,
They tear down tolerance and build separating walls,
So they can claim they have no equals.

They can only stay at the top,
With the help of those who would make the balloon pop,
So, stop lifting up those with mindless moral rot.

And start giving the underestimated, humble, and meek, a shot.

Upload of fear and anger?

The political rhetoric is never ending,
It goes in circles fanning the flames it's tending.

Violent coups to disrupt an election,
Sham recounts and lawsuits to coerce the corrupt correction.

Right wing fear mongering makes it impossible for half to see,
The difference between peaceful civil rights and
    race riots, properly.

Civil servants on both sides demonized for doing their job,
Smearing them all, gives the dishonest ones free rein
    to gain power and rob.

They can't be held accountable because the institution
    has been undermined,
By years of distrust in dirty politicians and the system,
    they opined.

They told you they all were dishonest, greedy, and opportunistic,
Using it to purge the fictional deep state, as if it were realistic.

They bully by character smearing and ideologically
    shaming those with morals,
When evil does their bidding they laugh and sit back
    on their laurels.

Now they want to teardown the progress and blissfully go back,
They even smear family and friends who defend the
    unAmerican attack.

On democracy, human rights, and humanity itself,
They wait for the end, buy guns, and horde supplies from
    the shelf.

It's getting very near the end when rhetoric has more power
    than a friend,
Even love and tolerance is seen as a threat against which
    they must defend.

When facts have no meaning because they come from
    the other side,
Objectivity is offensive to those trying to divide.

They can not defend with reason so they must declare
    cultural superiority,
Based in belief, there is no relief from their contempt
    for the majority.

Ideological bullies

They character smear, shame, and eventually threaten.
Even against their friends and family, their hearts will batton.

No evidence or thought provoking question can
    make them budge,
Against the conspiratorial ideology they have chosen to
    obsessively love.

Grooming started early, the conditioning was thorough,
To feel special as a white Christian American capitalist,
    an identity that is shallow.

Empathy is hard to feel for those socialists, when you've been
    told you are superior.
You hear they are lazy, leachy, or have values which are inferior.

Because your views rationalize your selfishness.
And your beliefs are the foundation of your self esteem
    and worthiness.

You must push those away who bring overwhelming evidence
    to the contrary.
Scientific evidence is a threat to your very self esteem that
    you hold primary.

Don't present evidence to the contrary or they will
    vitriolically scold,
Doesn't matter how overwhelming, they can't see through
    the ideological blindfold.

The sociopath wraps their ego in belief, so as not to be offended
    by truth and facts.
Political ideology and religion makes them justified in
    their hostile acts.

Can we reach them with love, can we remove the blindfold
    with reason?
Or will they keep projecting a war on their culture,
    justifying unlawful sedition.

Well if you don't accept Jesus Christ you are going to hell?
How is that ringing tolerance's bell?

Paranoid because someone may take your ability to quickly
    exterminate humans?
Over 370 million and growing with mental disorders
    and desperate problems?
Yea! Give them all guns!!!!

If a doctor recommends, or a woman decides on abortion,
    they are baby killers?
When voting against healthcare, welfare, and education
    for breathing babies, are your pillars?

You pretend to respect other faiths, while you cry there is
     a war on Christianity?
Maybe you should stop pretending American Christian
     exceptionalism IS morality.

Then we can begin to listen, respect and love ourselves as equals.
Instead of putting faith in ideological bullies who make us feel,
     "the specials."

They would rather put a gun in your hand, than a ballot,
If you keep talking that way, they suggest you might get shot.

By a 2nd amender?
A real patriotic populist pretender?

It's not enough to let the victims, minorities, and meek
     get bullied,
We must all stand up for one other, for all human rights
     around the world are married.

Both siderism

"There are good people on both sides."
One working toward democracy, the other goosesteps
    in ideological strides.

Do good people stand by those who threaten genocide?
Do good people, when they don't get what they want,
    threaten homicide?

Do good people let children walk around with weapons of war?
Do good people only let the privileged walk through their door?

Do good people make walls to horde their prosperity?
Do good people defend, with lethal force, their materialistic
    property?

Do good people try to get others to forget about the evils
    of the past?
Do good people ignore structural racism because it makes
    them feel bad, in contrast?

Do good people think their beliefs are more valid than facts?
Do good people use threats of fear and violence to justify
    their selfish acts?

No, both sides do not lie, cheat, and steal,
This is the both siderism, evil would like you to believe is real.

As long as a sizable population subscribes to this amoral ideology,
Interactions will be tribal, intolerant, and based
    on supremist mythology.

You can't bring heaven to earth with a gun,
Until we realize this, both siderism WILL be the poison.

Social Memory Complex vs Individual Identity

Could you imagine a world where people could agree
    on a foundation of facts?
Where science, history, and common sense were not
    under attack?

Could you imagine an entire human race working together
    to end suffering?
Unselfish benevolent humans extending kindness
    and understanding.

What would be the cost of putting down our weapons we
    point at each other?
Would evil conquer the world for selfishness, or could we
    lift up one another?

What would be the cost of giving up beliefs of spiritual
    and ideological superiority?
Could we give up comforting myths and accept
    our ignorance humbly?

Could you accept a future in which your party, religion,
    or country is not in control?
Could you accept a future in which the homeless, meek,
    and poor, are people we extol?

Or will we continue to worship selfishness and raise up
the greedy?
Giving them privilege and worship for their ability to take
from the needy.

Should we gain wealth from taking or giving to others?
Will we worship extortionists winning at capitalism,
for misleading their sisters and brothers?

Can we continue to claim that the individual, their race, tribe,
or culture is superior?
Making everyone else the enemy or competitor, is a species
hampering behavior.

So much wasted energy, time, and capitol on the acquisition
of power,
Selfish energy which could have strengthened humanity,
as a whole to empower.

If we continue to twist reality, to selfishly hold power
for ourselves,
It will come at the cost of taking compassion, reason,
and tolerance off the shelves.

In America

In America, I am expected to use my Christian White Male
    superiority,
It helps maintain the system, while I lose the majority.

If I reject it, I reject the system, for which my family and friends,
    are apart,
They would feel offended, rejected, accused of evil, a hardening
    of heart.

I am fearful of this, so I make sure to not speak out,
There are always others who are crazier and have a louder shout.

If you choose to educate, help, or represent them all,
They will demonize you as a leach, a big hearted screwball.

I am expected to carry a gun, just in case they rob,
I know, because right wing news, repeatedly, shows
    the violent liberal mob.

I rely more on belief more than I do on science and civics,
Because OUR leaders tell us the truth, and scientists are
    in the libs pockets.

Everything the left does is a conspiracy against
    western civilization,
I know because they tell me every night, on my
    white-is-right wing television.

Every night they show how our culture, society, and country
    is dying,
They even have a war on our religion, white Jesus is crying.

In America, It's every man, woman, and child for themselves,
Our leader said, "It's going to be wild!"
So it's time we all brace ourselves.

MOB MENTALITY

Did they lie to make you upset?
So much, you gave them your wallet?

Did they tell you your job was on the line?
Did they tell you liberalism was a crime?

Did they tell you immigrants were violent?
Did they tell you democracy was sleeping silent?

Did they tell you all the politicians were bad?
Did this make you hopeless and mad?

Did you get together with others fomenting the lie?
Were you chanting slogans and shouting, liberty or die!

When they told you where to direct your anger, then disappeared,
It never occurred to you? That the law, for them, is tiered?

They won't pay the price for fomenting your violence,
No one around you ever asked if it made sense.

They were seeing red, and wanted someone to pay,
They just didn't know it was themselves, that day.

2paths

There are two paths. Service to self or service to others,
Is there a balance? Or are they both in an epic fight for powers?

Maybe they are in a dance of married movement?
Selfishness and Selflessness swirling in complimentary
  commitment.

One is for love, the other is for contempt,
Each one trying to make the other nonexistent.

But where only one exists, the other would not,
How would you know one, if the other was forgot?

This is the struggle between yin and yang,
That began at the very big bang.

Most of us walk up and down the confluence, never getting far,
Opportunistically strolling between caring and the wine bar.

Only the most devoted can reach the end of each path,
One is paved with compassion, the other, with wrath.

It is why pure egotistical capitalism can not sustain,
And why communism is not easily maintained as humane.

It is why mixed economies work to maintain the balance,
Between human greed and government socialism,
    in a democratic existence.

Together or not at all.

If you want to save black lives, you are going to have to
    save the whites.

If you want to save women, you will have to save the men.

If you want to save the children, you will have to save the adults.

If you want to save yourselves against desperate human acts,
    you will have to save the complacent.

If you want to save your strong country, you will have to
    save weaker ones.

If you want to save human rights, you are going to have to
    save the refugees.

If you want to save the humans, you will have to save the earth.

If you want to save yourselves, you will have to save others.

It's not complicated but against our nature,
To help others instead of gaining from forces we capture.

What do we have to give back to this universe?
Why should it allow us to consume continuous?

If we only take from others and our home,
We will be left in a garbage heap biome.

That is why it is important we save each other,
Instead of enriching yourself, by taking from
    your sister and brother.

Because it is together, or not at all,
Together we stand strong against challenges, or divided we fall.

GOD

Some people say they can't see god, and therefore it doesn't exist,
But they can't see the beauty in front of their eyes, they missed.

Everything you see is a manifestation of the multiverse,
It's quite unique and nothing is destined or rehearsed.

Everything in existence is a part of GOD, you see?
You, me, and everything you can and can not see.

It exists apart from you, but also within,
A spirit, an energy, something you just can't pin.

Billions of particles and atoms spinning around,
But to us, it just looks like an ordinary stone on the ground.

The infinitely beautiful can look mundane,
To an animal who can't conceptualize the profane.

So many people travel to the ends of the earth,
Some worship on specific days, in their peoples' church.

But, It is not belief which will connect you with it,
It is not faith which will keep your fire lit.

You need to wake up and look what is right in front of you,
You were given everything already, you know all you need to do.

Just be thankful for space and time,
So I can give service to others with lives meeker than mine.

Cognition Recognition

If you experience;
Suffocation,
Hunger,
Thirst,
Oppressive heat,
Freezing cold,
Physical pain,
Exhaustion,
Or any other depravity of bodily functions,
You will feel the most primal of emotions,
You will display selfish and immoral, animalistic passions.

If you experience,
Houselessness,
Unemployment,
Immorality from those you trust,
Ailing health,
Or stolen prosperity,
You will feel the disparity of inequity,
You will feel resentment for those born to secured social security,
You will feel the sting of poverty, in a society with
    money amorality.

If you experience;
Lack of prejudice,
Caring friends,
A supportive family,
And a loving personal intimacy,
You will feel the belongingness of love's potent efficacy,
You will feel hope in a community of communal advocacy.

If you experience;
Self worth,
Self assurance,
Knowledge/Wisdom,
Successes,
And respect from others,
You will feel a sense of accomplishment and pride,
You will be able to deal with complications in stride.

You will feel whole, activated, and . . . well . . . good!
You will lift up others and do what you should,
In order to make heaven on earth understood.

So be conscious of the way others may be experiencing life,
Just because you live bougie,
doesn't mean others aren't suffering from suffocating strife.

You might be able to rationalize your success and push
    the unsavory images away,
But, suffering in society makes us morally impoverished,
    everyday.

Economic thievery

Taking from others has always been an economic system,
But, is it built into the human condition?

From the very first feelings of banana envy,
Did we feel embarrassment, then turn it into an angered frenzy?

From tribal raids to gain wealth and women,
Did it make us feel better to comfort ourselves from
    such sufferin?

One tribe would enslave the other,
Building powerful nations for others to envy in wonder.

Great wars and projects were fueled through forced labor,
Giving the elite a place to carve their names forever.

Although the names have been forgotten,
We must not forget the lives that were taken.

We must not forget the greed mixed with brutality,
that allowed people to profit from economic inhumanity.

It is unsustainable because of the human condition,
To survive and thrive regardless of the starting position.

We think we are superior to other animals, all the time,
Then why can't we overcome our greedy violence with
    the sublime.

To provide service to others weaker and poorer than ourselves,
Is something American culture has largely put on the shelves.

We have tried philanthropy, and half measured socialism,
But until living is a right,
Economic thievery will continue, in the name of capitalism.

Putin and You

Would you like to restrict the lives of those who are gay?
And make it unsafe for them on a public walkway?

Would you like to arrest liberals who speak out?
Sending fear through those who would support a peaceful route?

Do you secretly wish the worst for your political rivals?
Dreams of assassinations, executions, and civil servants
    in shackles?

Would you like to outlaw mainstream media (free press)?
Because it gives unbiased data against your megalomania?

Do you think international concepts of human rights
    are restricting?
Do they shame you for the suffering child refugees you
    are rejecting?

Does environmentalism restrict your power and money flow?
Because you reject the data of world calamity, scientists show?

Do you want to make your country great again?
From progressive historical reality you abstain.

Do you praise nationalists and dictators for their strength?
While denigrating democracy at arms-length?

Do you selectively pick parts of Christianity to justify actions?
Then demonize peaceful protesters, protesting
    unjust transgressions.

If you are so afraid of conflict you smear civics as political,
    and avoid it to be comfortable,
Someone will gladly take that right from you, and it won't
    be equitable or debatable.

If this sounds like something you would like to impose
    on yourself and others,
Then Putin is for you. He will solve all of your answers,
    as humanity shudders.

Thank you for getting to the end of this journey with me. There is nothing greater than teaching humanity to be better, kinder, gentler, smarter, and more tolerant to the universe . . . which includes ourselves. My hope is that by reading and writing these poems, I can help humanity explore and examine our hardware and software more closely. By analyzing our deepest subliminal programing, we can be more mindful and purposeful in our actions. The result, I hope, is a more positive future for our families, country, and entire world.

"Omnia vincit amor, et nos cedamus amori!"
Virgil, Eclogues

www.ingramcontent.com/pod-product-compliance
Lightning Source LLC
Chambersburg PA
CBHW060310100426

42812CB00003B/724

9 781666 774115